THE WILLIAMS FAMILY

Presents

4 Seasons of Love

By: K. Moore

Copyright © 2024 by K.Moore

All rights reserved. No part of this book may be used or reproduced in any form whatsoever without written permission except in the case of brief quotations in critical articles or reviews.

This book is a work of fiction. Names, characters, businesses, organizations, places, events and incidents either are the product of the author's imagination or are used fictitiously. Any resemblance to actual persons, living or dead, events, or locales is entirely coincidental.

Printed in the United States of America.

For more information, or to book an event, contact :
relatablefictionwriting.com
http://www.relatablefictionwriting.com

Book design by (Nakeia Davis)
Cover design by Canva)

First Edition: May 2025

Dedication

1 Cor 13:4

Love is patient, Love is kind, Love is not jealous. Love does not brag or boast, it does not get puffed up with pride

1

(Winter)December 2028

Here we are ending 2028 and entering 2029 time to Live, Laugh and Love. Let's begin at the start of Dec 1, 2028 to see what all of our couples are doing for the next 90 days. One thing is for sure and that's the fact that we'll be planning Christian and Desiree's wedding. I know in Bonded by Love we said the wedding would be in 2032 but Kahlani can't wait that long to see her son happily wed.

Before we start I want to let you know that some of the fun activities in this book will be expanded on in the next book. So let me wet your appetite for **(M.A.) Marriage Anonymous**. With that being said let's dive right into **4 Seasons of Love**.

Dec 1 was an ordinary day for Zeek and Kahlani who went to their Sunday meeting. After hearing a talk about forgiveness which made Zeek think of his former comrade Jamal Reynolds. When he got home Zeek called his boss asking what happened to Jamal. The Chief replied: Jamal was released 3 yrs ago and has been laying low in Virginia.

Speaking of Jamal I heard he asked you (Zeek) to raise his kids while he was locked. Yeah Chief he did ask me and so did Melody and Destiny. But I need to track him down because he's in the same state as his son and hasn't laid eyes on him yet, Zeek replied. The chief gave a heartfelt response saying: I think you should find him since his birthday is in 12 days and he should at least spend it with his kids.

After hanging up the phone Zeek was dumbfounded at the thought of a man becoming a father at 37 and not knowing his children. Secondly, how bad that man must feel living in the same state as one of his children and not know it. Zeek didn't know what he'd do if he had children who didn't know who he was. As a father it was on his heart to reunite his former colleague with his children. Next he called Rashad and Max to tell them his plan. Rashad asked before hanging up if this was Zeek's way of forgiving Jamal? Yeah man was all that Zeek had to say for his friends to agree to help.

Since police work is all Jamal knew how to do Zeek spent the next 8 days calling every police department in Virginia. By the 10th day Max was the one to find Jamal working at the Antioch Police Station. Max put them on a 3-way call with Zeek who had one thing to say to Jamal. "Come back to Richfield to see your daughter" and when you go back home stop by 2453 South Caldwell St in Antioch to see your son.

With emotion in his voice Jamal replied: Zeek I thought you had my kids the whole time. Who has my kids? Are they in foster homes? No, your kids are fine. Max located Destiny's Aunt in Antioch who took your son in and daughter Harmony has shared custody of him with Aunt Ella. As for your daughter Melody's parents live across the street from me so they took custody of her. My son Malcolm is an officer now so he takes care of his little sister as well.

Happy to know that his children were being loved in his absence Jamal replied I'm on my way now before hanging up. That went well was all Max said before hanging up. Zeek turned to go into the kitchen where Kahlani was fixing dinner with the help of Camille and Ann Marie. Was something wrong honey was the question Kahlani posed to her husband? I just found out that Serenity and Harrison's father has been free for 3 yrs and he thought we had his children so he never looked for them.

His birthday is in 3 days and he's on his way here from Virginia to see his daughter as we speak. I gave him aunt Ella's address to go see his son as well. Putting her arms around his neck Kahlani gave Zeek a peck on the lips saying: are you going to give Jamal some parenting advice when he arrives? Nope, I'll let Malcolm and Harmony give him advice since they're parents now and those are their siblings.

But I wouldn't mind if you make me a daddy again, because you know I'm gonna keep trying until you do. No you're not gonna put another baby in me mister as she sashayed away from Zeek. Before he could respond Malcolm walked in the front door. He greeted everyone in the kitchen before saying: what's this I hear that my sister's dad is on his way here tonight? Zeek turned to him saying: yeah son he's out for 3 yrs and thought that I had custody of your sister and Harrison so he never bothered to look for them.

So what made him want to see them now? Malcolm asked, starting to get angry. It was my idea after the meeting I was wondering what he was up to since he should've been out by now. I called the chief and then I asked uncle Max and Rashad to help me track him down. Max called me on 3-way when he found him and I told him where the kids were. He lives and works in the same city where Harrison is being raised. Hearing this news made Malcolm get emotional, he understood Jamal's situation from a father's perspective since he also has a son.

An hour later at 6pm on Dec 10th the doorbell rang and on the other side was an emotional Jamal Reynolds. Both Malcolm and Zeek went to answer the door together so Kahlani could finish dinner. With tears in his eyes Jamal asked: is my daughter here with you man? Nah man she's not with me but Malcolm will take over to her home, he's headed over there before he calls it a night. After closing the front door Malcolm told Jamal they had to make a pit stop next door before going to Serenity.

The two men walked into Malcolm's home where he embraced his wife and a little boy. Malcolm turned around and introduced Kapri to Serenity's dad. Then he picked up the little boy asking him if he wanted to see Serenity? The joy on the child's face made Jamal emotional as a tear rolled down his cheek. Then Malcolm said Jamal this is my son Marquis to which Marquis replied I'm 3. When they arrived across the street they let Marquis knock on the door.

As the door opened Marquis ran in yelling , GG and PaPa where Serenity. When the now 8 yr old turned to corner Jamal was speechless, she looked just like Melody. She leaned over to give Marquis a kiss on the cheek before running over to hug her big brother asking: Mally, who is this man? This man is your daddy little sister. He came to see you and he's going to see Harrison too. Your daddy's birthday is in three days. Can he spend it with you? Malcolm asked with a sincere smile.

Serenity looked at her grandparents for confirmation to which they nodded yes. That sounds cool but I'm going to play with Marquis right now. Mrs. Stanton turned to Jamal saying: you can stay in the guestroom if you'd like. Spend your birthday with her and earn her trust. After hearing that Jamal agreed, grabbed his things from his truck and settled in. For the next 2 days the two made breakfast together and Serenity even asked Jamal to take her and pick her up from school.

Then **Dec 13th** came and Serenity wanted to stay home with her dad but he said no. When he dropped her off to school she asked him to walk her to class. As they arrived at the classroom Serenity announced "today is my dad's birthday and he's a policeman just like my brother". The whole class clapped and sang to him before he turned to leave heading back to the house. Sitting in the living room Jamal was overcome with emotion that his 7 yr old daughter has accepted him into her life. Here he was at 45 starting from scratch at everything (career, parenting, friendship etc).

When he picked Serenity up from school she asked Jamal if they could go to the rec center. He couldn't tell his princess no, so he spent his 45th doing whatever would put a smile on his daughter's face. By the weekend Jamal had to break the sad news to Serenity that he'd be leaving to go back to work. The look of sadness on her face broke Jamal's heart but he promised to take her to his house for winter break in a week and a half.

Just as he promised Jamal came back on Dec 23rd to pick Serenity up for a visit to his home. Before leaving they went over to Malcolm's house where Jamal promised to take good care of her for him. They drove the 2 hr drive back to Virginia and stopped at the address Zeek gave for Harrison. After hearing 3 knocks on the door Aunt Ella opened the door to find Serenity and a man she didn't recognize. Serenity spoke up saying: This is my daddy, he wanted to meet us for his birthday. They went in to explain everything to Harrison.

2 days later on **Dec 25th** Harmony was still sleeping warm in bed. Meanwhile Travion and Heaven were in the kitchen making breakfast. Once the pancakes and bacon and eggs were done the two crept quietly up the stairs to the master bedroom. Upon entering the room Heaven shouted "Happy 5th Anniversary" waking Harmony up. After the family of three had breakfast in bed Trey and Heaven washed dishes before she went back to bed.

When he returned to the room Trey found his wife laughing on the phone with of all people Janette. That woman has an issue with everyone she meets in life. As he slid into bed with Harmony she put the call on speaker and Trey couldn't contain his laughter. Janette was telling us about how she almost slapped the sales lady at the mall over toys for Marquis and Heaven. "If only Heaven wasn't sleeping right now" Travion and Harmony thought as they listened to Janette's story. Both of the kids are three, how much trouble can a great-grandma get into buying toys for three yr olds?

After listening to the story we decided to stay in until the family arrived for dinner. Even though we don't celebrate the holidays, we do celebrate togetherness with our family and friends. By 6pm Janette and PopPop arrived with trays of food from their home. Once everyone arrived Camille took all the kids to play while the adults set the table. "Kids come eat," Kahlani exclaimed from the bottom step.

When all the kids got seated PopPop led us in prayer then "Oh Lord help us" Jsnette started with another hilarious story. We all looked at PopPop who was shaking his head as he took a bite of his fried chicken. After Janette finished telling us about her almost getting into a fight at the gym with her personal trainer over the trainer's fee. We understand that the fees are too high for anyone to afford.

Grandma, why are you going to the gym when everyone has gym equipment at home ? Just use PopPop's equipment in the basement, Christian asked? To be honest with you grandson,I was trying to get into better shape for my 7 yrs anniversary coming up that's why I did it, Janette replied. Janette, Jean and I workout together everyday and it's so therapeutic for us too, Ramona answered.

We hold hands taking the dog for a walk on the beach twice a day. We go bicycling and even take boxing classes together,

Jean stated smiling at Ramona. All the kids started asking if they could go to their house to help Janette get in shape. This is the best anniversary ever Harmony thought looking around the table. Now this is how you end one year to start another.

In a house filled with Love and Laughter all throughout. Especially if you have someone like Janette in your circle to make Life worth living. After 3 hours with the family everyone was ready to go to bed, so we cleaned up and called it a night. Thank you readers for celebrating with us, Good night from Travion and Harmony Smith. See you guys next year.

2

January 2029

It's a new year and our favorite officer turns 45 today **Jan 1, 2029**. Zeek is bringing in the new year with his family and friends. Upon waking up he was greeted by the smiling faces of his twins holding a tray consisting of belgium waffles with sausage links and scrambled eggs. Brandon and Ann Marie joyfully replied "Morning Daddy here's your breakfast, we already ate and mommy has your juice". Uh Huh, we didn't want to spill it, Brandon proclaimed.

After the kids went to their room to play, Zeek and Kahlani had breakfast in bed. Then Kahlani leaned over to kiss her hubby before telling him to enjoy his day off. Then she took the tray to the kitchen to wash dishes before coming back to bed. Zeek turned to his wife pulling her close and asking " what are you going to do today beautiful"? With a smile she said " I'm going to start planning the wedding with Dsiree, then I'll be home in time to make dinner for MY husband".

"Oh and the kids want to go to Malcolm's house so I'll drop them off on my way to see Desiree", Kahlani mentioned as she went to her walk-in closet. That's fine with me, Zeek replied with a smile. About 45 minutes later he was alone in the house so he called Max and Rashad to come over. An hour later the guys arrived with Pizza, wings and some beers ready to watch some football. Just before kickoff for the Cowboys v Chiefs game the doorbell rang. On the other side of the door stood Chelsea Walters, one of the dispatchers from the station who had a crush on Zeek since he started his career as an officer.

"Chelsea why are you at my house", Zeek asked in confusion of seeing her at his home. The Chief told me it was your birthday so I came over to hang out, Chelsea answered flirtatiously hoping to be alone with Zeek. Chelsea, everyone in this city as well as the station knows I'm a happily married man, what makes you think I'd cheat on my wife in my own house with you nonetheless, Zeek asked? Besides, the game is about to start and I already have company to watch the game with me before closing the door in her face.

When she turned around completely humiliated Chelsea found herself face to face with Janette, Cora and Regina. Before she could say anything Janette hit her upside the head with the box that was holding a huge cupcake for Zeek. And quietly Regina and Cora dragged Chelsea away to her car where they told her to leave their friend's husband alone and not to try anything with their husbands either. Once she was gone the ladies left to go back home while Janette went to go get her son another cupcake.

Meanwhile over at Christian's house Kahlani was sitting at the dining room table asking Desiree what type of venue she wanted for the wedding. Desiree was about to describe the venue she wanted when her cell rang and Kapri's name came across the screen. Hey girl ma is over here helping me put this wedding together, Desiree stated with a smile looking over at her mother in-law to be. I'm over here doing two heads of hair while Malcolm took the boys to the barber but if you need me to do anything don't hesitate to call me, Kapri replied. I sure will sister in-law, Desiree answered before hanging up. Then Desiree pointed out a couple places she wanted to look at for the wedding but they couldn't get an appointment to view them until March.

Eight days later Harmony and Heaven got up early to set up a scavenger hunt at the Smith home. It's **Jan 9, 2029** and our boy Travion is 25 today. When opened his eyes it was 8 am and his bed was empty except for a note on Harmony's pillow.

Morning Handsome,

I know you miss me and I miss you too
But not as much as our baby down the hall
Take 25 steps to my next clue for you
Our little princess has a gift that will make you feel 10 ft tall
Harmony

Travion threw on some sweats and went towards Heaven's room where she was standing in the doorway smiling up at him. Here's your next clue daddy, Heaven happily said as she handed over a box with a blue bow. Inside the box was another note from Harmony.

Hey hubby,

I love our family of 3 and we've been talking about growing our family tree
In the kitchen is where you'll find your gift with me in the oven
Love you hubby

                                                       Harmony

After reading that note I feel 10 times more confused than 10 ft tall about this gift, Travion thought. Taking Heaven by the hand he made his way to the kitchen where Harmony was. As they entered the kitchen Harmony was placing plates of food out for them to enjoy. After placing Heaven in her booster seat at the table Trey walked over to his wife asking " what's this about something in the oven"? Go take a look for yourself hubby was Harmony's response with a wink.

Walking over to the stove Trey opened the oven door to find another note and a small rectangular box. Before opening the box Travion nervously read the note

Hi Daddy

We haven't met yet but we will in September when I am born. I can't wait to meet my big sister Heaven and you along with the rest of the family.

Your Son

In disbelief Travion looked in the box only to find a pregnancy test with two lines on it. "I'm gonna be a daddy again" was all Travion could say in between his tears. He couldn't wait to tell everyone in the family the great news. This was the best gift Travion had ever received other than his wife and daughter. 7 days later everyone met up at Malcolm and Kapri's home to hear the news of a new baby being added to the family.

Let's not forget that on **Jan 16, 2029** the first grandbaby of Zeek and Kahlani was turning 4. With all the excitement about Harmony's pregnancy, the little man got overlooked but didn't even mind. All Marquis wanted to do was play and show everyone his new toys. For the rest of the month all of the ladies of the family assisted in the planning of Christian & Desiree's wedding.

3

February 2029

Now we enter the month all of our couples enjoy the most out of the whole year and the end of the winter season of Love. The first week takes us to Desiree and her future mother in-law meeting with caterers for the wedding. Since it will be taking place in New Orleans it's only right to have a buffet-style reception. The bride wanted some gumbo on the menu as well. What do you think the guys are gonna do for us next week ma, Desiree asked Kahlani on the way home.

I don't know but I'm sure whatever they plan we'll all feel like royalty by the end of the day, Kahlani replied. A week later on **Feb 14,2029** all the ladies a day at the spa. All the men took the little ones to hang out while they planned the evening for the ladies. When each of the ladies got home they found notes left by their husbands asking them to meet in different places.

1) Since Desiree was turning 22 on this very day Christian planned a candle light dinner at the planetarium. In his note he asked his bride-to-be to meet him downtown by the Aquarium. She told him that she loved going to the aquarium. After walking around all the sea creatures Desiree said she was hungry. Christian led Desiree out of the Aquarium and down the street to the Planetarium for their dinner reservation.

2) Since they couldn't make it back to the states to visit and their home was on the beach Jean gave Ramona what she always appreciates. A trail of rose petals leading from their backdoor to the sandy beach where he stood waiting for her. Then the two had a picnic under the stars.

3) As we all know there's no way of keeping Janette relaxed in a public setting. But somehow Mike was able to take his wife skating which had them both smiling the whole night. First they went ice skating in the local park near their home. Then they went to the roller skating rink and bought some snacks before getting on the floor. Within 15 mins of skating a lady around their age approached and started flirting with Mike and of course y'all know Janette went off.

4) Zeek left Kahlani a note to meet him at the pier by 7pm. When she arrived there was her husband standing on a yacht with his hand outstretched. Taking

his hand Kahlani was helped onto the yacht while asking "baby why are we on a yacht"? We're going to have dinner down on the lower deck before going to our room, Zeek replied. Are we spending the night on this yacht, Kahlani asked with a flirty smile. Yes beautiful I rented this yacht for 13 hrs so we have it until 8 am tomorrow.

5) Dametrius decided to forgo the note and took Jazzlene to a pottery class during the afternoon, By the night the two chose to stay in and watch movies on RedBox after dinner.

6) Travion asked Harmony to meet him at the local library in his note. When she arrived Trey told her they were going to a book club meeting about the writings of her favorite author K.Moore. Hearing this Harmony ran into Trey's arms giving him a sweet kiss before making their way inside. 2 hrs later on the way home Harmony happily exclaimed " this has been the best date ever, can we come back again"? We sure can baby, Travion answered.

7) In his note Max requested that Cora meet him at the local art gallery. Little did Cora know Max has already purchased some of the art pieces that they viewed in their tour. At the end of the tour Max pointed out the pieces he'd purchased for their home saying "these paintings in the corner are going up in our home". They'll be delivered tomorrow at 4 pm.

8) Finally we have Rashad who asked Regina to meet him at the airport by 8 pm. He also hired a car service to

make sure she arrived on time. As she got out of the car she looked up at the helicopter asking Max why they were on the air strip. "Baby we're taking a helicopter ride getting a view of our city, Max replied". What a romantic way to end the day for these lovers.

The next morning on **Feb 15,2029** Jamal made his way back to Richfield, TN to see Serenity turn 8. While having dinner Jamal asked Mr & Mrs Stanton if he could take Serenity to VA for the weekend. These grandparents knew he was asking to celebrate the birthdays of his two children. Jamal you are her father as long as we know she is in safe hands we don't mind,Mrs.Stanton replied. Beaming with pride Jamal asked Serenity to pack a bag for the weekend.

On the way back to Antioch,VA Jamal called Zeek,Rashad and Max asking if they would bring their kids for the weekend? All of the men agreed and went to discuss it with their wives who thought it was a great idea. Two days later on **Feb 17th** Jamal and Serenity picked Harrison up from aunt Ella's home. Back at Jamal's house the brother and sister ran to their designated rooms and were amazed at everything their father bought them. All the age appropriate toys and books made them smile which in turn made Jamal feel good in his heart.

For so long Jamal didn't feel like he would be able to be a good enough father to his children. Maybe he should've asked Zeek for some advice since he's been a dad longer than any of the other men in this series. But at this very point

Jamal is just happy to see his children happy and having fun.

Meanwhile back in Richfield a week later on **Feb 25th** our former police chief Michael Joseph Byrd turns 69. What could his wife possibly have in store for him? For starters Janette decided to surprise Mike with a weekend getaway for the two of them. And she promised to behave this time, there's no need for how she acted on their honeymoon. Janette rented a quaint log cabin air bnb in the mountains for the weekend. Before getting on the road they stopped to buy some groceries since Janette had packed nearly all of her spice cabinet to take with them.

After checking in the two had a quiet dinner together before going to bed for the night. The next morning Janette made her hubby breakfast in bed then they got dressed to go do some sightseeing in the mountains. The couple decided to go snow tubing and that's where the drama begins. The attendant was flirting with Mike telling him that she'll get in the tube with him while his wife would be too heavy. And that Janette should ride in a tube by herself. Offended by the whole conversation and before Mike could respond to the lady's comment y'all Janette slapped the girl so hard. The impact was so hard that she slid head first down the hill still holding the tube in her hand.

Everyone that was watching started videoing that attendant while looking on in shock. Janette and Mike got into another tube and went down the slope passing the attendant who was begging for someone to help her. By the next day it was all over social media with captions such as " I thought penguins couldn't fly but they do today". Before they went back to their cabin Mike wanted to stop at a souvenir shop to look around. When they got to the register the young lady recognized them and was instantly scared of Janette.

The young lady thought Janette wasn't paying attention when she slipped her number in the bag for Mike to call her. Before they could pull off Janette went back into the store and handed the girl her number back. Just as Janette was walking out the door she left the girl with some advice. If you think slapping that attendant down that slope was harsh, I'll slap you harder for thinking my husband will ever call you. Oh and another thing you may want to hand your number to someone that's single and in your age bracket next time.

Back in the car Mike asked Janette what took place in the store. Bracing himself for another hilarious story to tell the family Michael left the vehicle in park. Janette told him simply "I told her to slip her number to someone single and her age, so she won't encounter someone like me that'll slap her off the mountain instead of just a ski slope". Shaking his head Mike drove back to the cabin to get some sleep before checking out in the morning.

When they were driving home Mike could tell Janette wanted to start telling everyone about their trip. Once they were unpacked Mike told her to wait until the family came over to talk about it. A week later the family arrived to visit with the grandparents. Harmony asked how their weekend getaway was. Everyone noticed PopPop was laughing in the corner so they knew the story was going to be a good one. In dramatic fashion Janette started telling the story as only she could.

Within 15 mins everyone including the kids were bent over in a fit of laughter. Janette was the only one not laughing as she stated "I told y'all these heifers out here are thirsty to find themselves a sugar daddy" but not a single man with money. They want a married man with money to take care of them but those two learned this weekend. Nobody will be taking money out of my house, not out of his pension or out of my social security. You can and will get hurt for trying.

4

(Spring)March 2029

On **Mar 5, 2029** Max and Cora's triplets turned 6 and are enjoying 1st grade. On the way home they asked if they could go to the trampoline park on the weekend. This was music to Cora's ears so she ran to call everyone about the play date. As the weekend rolled around all the men decided to invite Jamal to play basketball while the kids were at the trampoline park. Meanwhile at the park Kahlani talked to all the ladies about helping Desiree look at Ceremony spaces. After 4 hrs all of the kids were now tired so it was time to head home.

The next day **Mar 6th** our boy Christian turns 22 and his bride-to-be left him a sweet little note on the nightstand.

Morning Handsome,

I can't wait to become your wife in 4 months so I wanted to let you know how excited I am. Go out on the back porch to see clue number 1 and I hope you have fun

Desiree

Upon opening the back door Christian found a picture of a star constellation and another note.

Christian

I'll be in class for most of the day but can you meet me at the planetarium by 6pm. I have something to show you and ask you there

Desiree

After reading that note Christian spent the rest of his day off relaxing at home. All the while wondering what Desiree could have in store for him that evening. By 5:50 Christian walked into the planetarium looking for Desiree. At 6pm on the dot Chritian found his lady standing under a star constellation in the shape of a heart. With tears in her eyes Desiree asked Christian "can we have the wedding right here, it's perfect Please". Of course we can queen, Christian replied as a table for two was set up for them to eat dinner.

Now with the Ceremony space secured Kahlani enlisted the ladies to help find a reception space for Christian and Desiree. While out with the girls Regina saw a firetruck Lincoln asked for last year, it was on sale for 70% off. Then she announced that Lincoln will be 5 in a week on **Mar 12th**. Are you and Rashad planning anything for my nephew,

Regina, Cora asked curiously?

Well we were planning to have a sleepover for all the kids if you guys are ok with it, Regina replied. I don't mind at all and Camille could help with the little ones, Kahlani said happily. Then all the ladies agreed. A week later all the little people were packed in the Lewis residence. For Regina this was a fun time but for Rashad all these kids in his house were major birth control for him.

Three days later **Mar 15th** Harmony turned 25 and was enjoying her pregnancy. While in her bed Heaven got into bed and rubbed her belly that was just starting to show. The whole day was spent out shopping with Travion and Heaven. Every store they passed Heaven wanted to look for something for her baby brother. This is the most loveable time I've ever spent with these two, Harmony thought to herself.

For the rest of the month Desiree dragged her future mother-in-law to four places for the reception. Each place had some flaws but ultimately Desiree chose to have the reception at The Richfield Arena-Stadium. Now there are 90 days left to find a decorator and DJ for the wedding.

5

April 2029

Now it's getting warmer outside as we enter the month of April but it's a little sad for Kahlani. On **Apr 2nd** of every year Kahlani finds herself crying at random. This particular day is the day that her father Marcus DeAndre Coleman would be 72 had he been alive. It hurts my heart to remember the things my father did to me, Kahlani thought to herself while sitting in the bay window. To some it may seem weird that I love and miss the predator that caused my childhood trauma but I do. Growing up without a male role model/father was terrifying but the thoughts of the abuse is worse.

Kneeling down in a prayer pose by the window, Kahlani began to speak to her deceased father in prayer.

Dear Heavenly father

I know you've seen all the things that have taken place in my life. I know that the dead know nothing at all as they are no longer a part of the world. I have forgiven Marcus in my heart for his actions all those years ago. The child in my heart Loves and misses my dad and hopes to see him again in the resurrection.

Amen

Kahlani thought she would've been over her childhood trauma as she got older. But the memories of what she did to her father make her emotional on this day every year. No child should have to take the life of their parents just to escape the pain. Coming home for his lunch break Zeek found his Queen in distress. No need for words Zeek went into the kitchen to make their meal of *Grilled Cheese & Potato Soup*. Re-entering the living room he sat the tray on the coffee table and went over to the bay window to pick Kahlani up.

Sitting with her in his lap Zeek fed his wife her lunch before eating his own. Before heading back to work Zeek placed Kahlani into bed and told her to rest. Then he made snacks for the kids and sent Malcolm a text.

Mal, can you pick up your brother and sisters today? Ma isn't feeling well today. I already made snacks for them that should hold them until I get home.

A week and a half later Cora awoke to her children and husband saying "Good morning Mommy". Looking around confused as to what was going on, she finally looked at the tray in Max's hands. It read *"Your 43 today"* then Cora remembered that today was **Apr 15, 2029 "tax day"**. Her next thought was Thank God Max filed his taxes early because she had procrastinated until today. After filing her taxes online Cora had a relaxing day with her family at the day spa.

Five days later it was now **Apr 20,2029** and Kapri awoke to the faces of her two favorite men Malcolm and Marquis. While having breakfast Marquis decided to tell Kapri a secret. Mommy guess what me and daddy left you a present at work ok, I can't say anymore because daddy just said it's a surprise. Ok baby,mommy can't wait to see the surprise,Kapri replied with a smile. Since it was Malcolm's day off he decided to spend the day with his son and be his wife's chauffeur for the day.

Pulling up to the shop Kapri gave both men a hug and kiss before heading to her station. All the other stylists were shouting "Happy Birthday" but all Kapri was focused on was her station. A bouquet of white lilies with a note card was the first to catch her eye.

Hey beautiful

These lilies are to show how much you shine in my eyes.

Marquis and I have an evening of family fun planned for you. Have a great day we'll see you when we pick you up

Mal

Then she looked at the family portrait Marquis had made and the tears started to fall. I'm such a lucky woman, she thought to herself just before noticing the photo stuck on her mirror. It was a selfie of the three of them taken in January when Marquis turned 4. This is the start of the best day ever for Kapri and all her clients wanted to talk about the great man she had. By 5pm Malcolm pulled up to the curb and let Marquis out the back seat. Just as Kapri finished with her last client Marquis ran to her station shouting MOMMY getting everyone's attention.

Did you like your presents from me and daddy, Marquis asked looking up at his mom? I loved them baby and I love you and daddy too, Kapri said with a smile. We got more presents for you at home mommy "Let's Go" he shouted happily pulling Kapri toward the exit. Walking into the house Kapri announced that it smelled really good there. "I helped daddy and grandma make dinner for you mommy" Marquis exclaimed with glee. After putting away their shoes and jackets the family of three sat down for dinner. Plates of mashed potatoes, broccoli and turkey wings were on the table.

Once dinner was over Kapri went to get Marquis washed up and into bed noticing he was nodding off at the table.

Malcolm stopped her saying "meet me in the living room when you're done upstairs". Malcolm cleaned up the kitchen and waited 10 mins for Kapri to come down. When she appeared Malcolm was standing by the couch with two glasses of wine handing her a glass. Pulling her into him Malcolm replied "I hope you enjoyed this day baby".

Of course I did Malcolm it was the best day ever, other than marrying you and having Marquis, Kapri answered looking up into his eyes. Sitting the wine glasses on the table Malcolm kissed his wife replying "Good because it's not over yet" and carried her upstairs to their room. There was a bubbly bath ready for her then Malcolm tucked his queen into bed for the night.

Just 5 days later was none other than Malcolm & Kapri's 5th wedding anniversary on **Apr 25, 2029**. This day was filled with a picnic in the park for the two while Marquis was in daycare. Then the two love birds went to take a couples painting class. After picking Marquis up from daycare they went home for dinner. Again Malcolm cleaned the kitchen while Kapri tucked Marquis into bed. This time he told Kapri to meet him in their room instead of the living room when she was done.

To her surprise the room was decorated just as their room was on their honeymoon. A trail rose petals leading from the door to both the bed and bath tub. And a handsome husband in nothing but a pair of boxer briefs awaiting her arrival.

6

May 2029

Now we come to the end of the spring season of Love and it's a sweet one too. We begin on **May 8, 2029** where our favorite middle school teacher Kahlani turns 43 today. All the phone calls from family and friends made her heart so full. But the evening with her husband and kids was the most fun. Zeek decided to pull out the karaoke machine to let their little ones share in the fun.

After two hours of Camille, Ann Marie and Kahlani singing their hearts out it was time for bed. Brandon sat next to his dad saying "You sound amazing mommy". Thank You baby boy now it's time for bed let's head upstairs, Kahlani replied. Camille being the big helper she helped tuck her siblings into bed before heading to her room for the night. Finally alone in their room Zeek and Kahlani called it a night wrapped in a tight embrace.

Six days later Kahlani received a call from her mother asking what she could do for a 71 yr old man. It took a second but Kahlani realized it was **May 14th** and chef Jean's birthday. With a chuckle Kahlani replied"ma calm down and let's brainstorm a bit". What does PaPa like to do in his spare time on the island? Well he goes fishing, he loves to cook, he likes building things around the house, Ramona states. Ma how about you get some of the guys on the island to build him a workshop. Since your anniversary is coming up, maybe he could help the guys build the workshop.

Oh Lani you are a genius I'll get right on it when I get off the phone. We do have enough land to build it on and maybe even a guest house for the family, Ramona said excitedly. Once their call ended Ramona called the construction company to get started. When Jean got home from working at the restaurant Ramona told him about the idea Kahlani gave her earlier. It was no surprise Jean loved the idea and couldn't wait to get started.

11 days later Malcolm turned 29 on **May 25th** and was in for a big surprise from his wife. After breakfast and taking Marquis to daycare the husband and wife made their way home. Once in the house Kapri went to her master closet to get the box holding Malcolm's surprise. She took a seat next to Malcolm on the bed and handed him the box with a mischievous smile. Looking into the box Malcolm found a note card that read:

Hi Daddy

Mommy just found out about me two days ago but you'll meet me when you turn 46 next year. Mommy will have a twin coming home to you and big brother. ILove you and can't wait to meet you.

Your little princess

Completely in shock Malcolm just stared at Kapri for a long moment. With teary eyes Kapri says " We're having a baby girl". Malcolm didn't even look at the pregnancy test in the box; he just scooped his wife up for a kiss. Then he leaned down whispering: daddy can't wait to hold you princess. That evening the two of them sat with Marquis to tell him the news and his excitement could be felt everywhere.Even when he was going to bed Marquis kissed his mommy's tummy saying: he has to kiss his sister good night.

Three days later on **May 28th** we have two wedding anniversaries taking place. Let's see what Max and Cora have planned for their 6 yr anniversary then we'll talk to Rashad and Regina. First thing in the morning Regina called Cora with an idea for their anniversaries. Cora, what do you think of us going to the movies and having dinner together, Regina asked. After 6 yrs I think that's a great idea girl: what movie should we go see, Cora replied. Girl since all of our kids will be at a sleepover with Kahlani and Zeek let's get some movies from redbox and order delivery to my house, Regina answered.

Friend, that's a great idea since Max and I don't get out much other than to do kid stuff. We appreciate you hosting us for "OUR" anniversary since we did get married on the same day. Next year we'll host you guys at our home for "OUR" anniversary. Later on into the evening Max and Cora arrived at the Lewis residence to hang out with their friends. 10 mins after arriving the doorbell rang and Cora turned around to answer the door.

On the other side of the door was a door dash driver with two bags of food from World Tavern. Max tipped the driver as Cora took the food to the kitchen. While fixing their plates Cora asked: What will we be watching and the guys will be hating? The guys like football so we'll watch "The Longest Yard" then we'll watch "Madea's Witness Protection". After both films were done Max and Cora made their way home.

Two days later on **May 30th** Zeek and Kahlani were having a barbeque which turned into a Block Party. The twins were also turning 8 along with it being their 10th wedding anniversary. Kahlani just wanted to see all the kids have fun and hang out with friends and family. From one end of the block to the other everyone was having a great time all day. That's how you get ready for the summer to arrive in the hood.

7

(Summer)June 2029

We're bringing in the Summer season with our favorite grandma Janette turning 68 on **June 5th**. At the house Mike had hired a private chef for the day just for her. Janette was so happy to be catered to by her husband in this manner. It made Mike proud to see his wife happy and not putting on a show. But we shouldn't get our hopes up when it comes to Janette at any given time.

By the end of the day after dinner as the chef was leaving Mike handed her a tip. The chef in turn handed Mike her number and address thinking Janette didn't notice. Y'all know Janette saw it and went from zero to 1000 in 2.5 seconds. Before Mike could hand it back to the chef Janette pushed him to the side and back-handed the lady. The lady's head hit the door frame so hard that she blacked out for a few seconds. When the lady came to the face looking down at her, it belonged to Janette who was holding a belt. Trying to crawl away from Janette the lady received a beating from an irate Janette. This went on all the way down the driveway until the lady got to her vehicle and drove away. Walking back into the house Janette opened the chef app and left a bad review of the chef that came to her home.

Four days after the comedy show we have Jazzlene turning 25 on **June 9th.** Dametrius invited the other couples to join them at the state fair for the day. Seeing all their friends and family out with her made Jazzlene want to share some news with everyone. Not even Dametrius knew what she was going to announce until she said: **I'm 2 months pregnant.** That means she's due around the same time as Kapri in 2030.

With all this love being spread throughout this family and all these pregnancy announcements. We haven't checked on Desiree since her wedding is in 3 weeks. At this point we have a ceremony space and a caterer in place. The reception space has also been chosen now a decorator needs to be hired. Our bride-to-be decided to let the groom worry about the DJ. Now she's resting and getting ready for the big day but she also has to pick up her dress.

Moving on to **June 29th** is the wedding anniversary of our favorite couple Zeek and Kahlani. To be honest they should have celebrated back in May but since the twins were born on their wedding anniversary so they'll celebrate today. Starting with breakfast with the kids before dropping them off at their brother's house. Then the husband and wife each went to get their hair freshly done. While Kahlani was letting Kapri style her hair a text popped up on her phone from Zeek.

Hey Beautiful

When you're done getting your hair done go get pretty for me. You've always been pretty in my eyes but tonight I want to see you look extra pretty. Then meet me at the airport at 7pm. The gift I have for you will blow your mind. See you later baby

Hubby

All the women in the salon began to swoon after looking at the message with Kahlani and Kapri. See y'all my husband is just like my father-in-law that's why we always look so happy all the time. We have the sweetest men in the city taking care of us, Kapri said happily. You got that right daughter-in-law we sure do, Kahlani replied. When she was finally done getting her hair done it was time to get a new outfit to meet her man.

Kahlani stopped at a new boutique in town to get some new threads for the night along with some new lingerie. As she walked through the store Jazzlene and Desiree were shopping as well. Saying hi to the girls Desiree asked for some advice on what lingerie to take on her honeymoon. After shopping with the girls it was time to go home to get dressed for her meeting with her hubby

Finally home, Kahlani looked at the clock and saw it said 5:30pm giving her 90 mins to get dressed and make it to the airport by 7pm. Once dressed, Kahlani walked outside to find a car service waiting for her at the curb. When they pulled up to the airport Zeek was standing next to a private jet. Looking charming in a pin-striped suit and a smile with a fresh cut and well manicured beard. After 10 yrs of marriage Kahlani never thought she'd be joining the mile high club but she will tonight.

Zeek helped his wife onto the jet and grabbed a blanket for their trip. Where are we going hubby, Kahlani asked with a flirtatious smile. We're going to Vegas for the weekend beautiful, Zeek replied with a wink. Overjoyed to know her husband was taking her somewhere she's never been had her smiling from ear to ear. As the jet taxied down the runway Kahlani snuggled up to her hubby until they were finally in the air. 3 hrs and 45 mins later the jet was landing in Nevada and another car service took them to a secluded house on the beach.

The house was filled with food for the couple to fix themselves the whole weekend. There was no need to go out for anything during their stay. Even the rose petals around the house let Kahlani know just how much time Zeek took to plan this anniversary trip. It was so peaceful to have some alone time from their jobs and their parental responsibilities.

Meanwhile on **June 30th** we have the anniversaries of Jean & Ramona and Mike & Janette. As we talked about in May, Ramona asked some guys on the island to help build a workshop for Jean. Now on their 7 yr anniversary she was able to show him the finished product today. In return he took his wife to the golf course. That was a request of hers all year even though Jean didn't think she needed to learn to play. That was something he did in his spare time but he's glad to share it with his wife.

While out on the course Ramona says: I wonder what Mike and Janette are doing for their anniversary. Whatever they're doing I'm sure it will end up being hilarious courtesy of Janette, Jean answered with a chuckle. I don't how many times we have said it but it needs to be said: I don't know how Mike keeps his sanity with that woman.

Back in Tennessee Janette and Mike were on their way to the Hyatt Grand Resort for the weekend. Once they checked in and entered their suite it was covered in red, white and yellow rose petals. What a beautiful start to a romantic weekend after 7 yrs of marriage. The romance didn't last long because by the time they went to dinner Janette thought the waitress was trying to shoot her shot with Mike.

In the blink of an eye Janette told the young lady to put her eyes back in her head and away from her husband. I know Mike had to be embarrassed at that table in front of all those other guests. By the time the restaurant manager arrived at the table Janette was irate. Janette explained how the server was flirting with Mike and she didn't like that. Then she said that she wanted the young lady fired for being inappropriate.

The manager didn't see any reason to fire the worker until the girl threw an alcoholic beverage in Janette's face. Before the man could say "Your Fired" Janette had picked the girl up and choke slammed her threw a table. Then Janette walked over to the manager and whispered in his ear: I'll pay to replace your table tomorrow and have our food delivered to suite 6945. Then she took Mike by the hand and walked to the elevator to go wait for their dinner. After having dinner and going to bed Mr & Mrs Byrd decided to stay in for the rest of their trip.

They got a couples massage in their room and no female masseuses were allowed in the room. All their room service was complementary for the rest of their trip as well. On Sunday it was time to check out and head home. As they arrived at the front desk everyone was afraid of Janette and shook their heads at poor Mike for having to put up with Janette. This was one heck of a way to start the summer guys but let's what else these couples have going on.

8

July 2029

Now we've finally made it to **July 4th** for Christian & Desiree's wedding day. First thing in the morning all the girls took Desiree to get her hair and nails done. All the guys were hanging out at the park, then to the gym, then to the barber. By 5pm it was time to head to the Planetarium for the wedding to begin. The Junior bridesmaid Camille wore Yellow *Chiffon one shoulder dresses* while the bride wore a White Satin *Trumpet dress with a Lace train.* All the men wore Black suits with Yellow bow ties and cumber buns.

Since all three of her bridesmaids were pregnant they wore Yellow *High neck Mesh dresses with Full Skirts.* Even the flower girl Heaven wore a Gold *Heart back Sequin Tulle Ball Gown.* Now you know we couldn't forget about the moms and grandmas wearing fabulous gowns. Kahlani dazzled in a Cream *Cap Sleeve Sheath Dress with Embellished waist.* Janette wore a beige *Embroidered Lace Sheath dress with Jacket.* While Desiree's mom wore a Lavender *Stretch Lace Off the shoulder Mermaid dress.*

It only took 45 mins for the ceremony then it was time for pictures before the reception. After pictures were done at the planetarium everyone made their way to the stadium for the reception except the bride and groom. The bride and groom went to the park for some more private photos and some alone time. Once they arrived at the stadium the whole place was a mixture of Mardi Gras and a Sreelers fan fare. Every inch of the place was covered in Black, Green and Yellow just as Desiree asked the decorator to do.

The buffet style dinner was a true southern feast for the ages for this family. Just before time to cut the four tier Black and Yellow cake Desiree decided to change. 10 mins later she returned in an Ivory *V-neck cap sleeve Midi dress with Fringe.* Now the party can begin and it was lit for the next 2 hours. As everyone made their way home at the end of the night, the newlyweds made their way to the airport. For the next 2 weeks they'll enjoy the sights and sounds of New Orleans and we'll check in on them a little later on.

7 days later on **July 11th** Dametrius turns 25 and is spending it with his mom and wife. The moment Jessica found out she was going to be a grandma she couldn't stay away from her son and daughter-in-law. Even today she came over to help us get the house ready for the baby. At this moment all Dametrius was focused on was putting together the crib in

the nursery. Jazzlene just went to the doctor 3 days ago now we know that we're having twins. I'm so excited to be a dad and promise to be a great father to my twins, Dametrius thought to himself.

In walks Jazz with her little baby bump asking if he needed any help with the crib. Sure baby I could use some help here since my mom just wants to announce to all her friends that she's gonna be a grandma instead of help. Then Jessica walked to the door of the nursery saying: I'll be moving for 3 months to help with my grandbabies when they're born. With that settled Mr & Mrs Stuart went on with putting together the crib.

Meanwhile over in New Orleans Christian and Desiree enjoyed the peace and quiet of their honeymoon suite. Not a care in the world until at night when people flood the streets . Going out onto the balcony they watched people dancing in the streets covered in colorful beads. All the room service was filled with delicious entrees that they wanted to imitate at home. Let's hope that this couple has a good loving marriage from here on out.

On **July 16th** and Roger Elias Williams would be 71 had he been alive. For Zeek it's a bittersweet moment every year around this month. Sitting in the bay window Zeek thought of what his life was like with Roger and how he wished things could've been different. He wished Roger could've been around to meet his grands and great-grands.

9

August 2029

Now we're at the end of the summer and let's start on **Aug 5th** with Ramona turning 71. After gifting Jean with a workshop he decided to make his wife a present. After taking Ramona for a walk on the beach Jean gifted her with a hand-made cutting board with their names engraved. On the fridge was a Heart magnet with ornate engravings of their family heritage. Overcome with emotion Ramona fell onto her husband's arms thanking him for his kindness repeatedly saying " I Love You so Much".

I Love You too Nani (beautiful) Jean replied with a kiss to the forehead and a hug. For the rest of the day these two cooked using the cutting board he made her. While enjoying their meal Ramona had to call Kahlani and tell her what Jean had made for her. PaPa, can you teach the guys to make gifts like that for us? Kahlani begged like a baby over the phone. I'd love to Kaikamahine (daughter), Jean replied.

Five days later on **Aug 10th** both Zeek and Malcolm sat at the cemetery in front of a headstone that read: **Melody Stanton.** Both men sat in deep thought of the woman they both loved in their hearts. Out of nowhere Zeek stated:Mal I loved your mother man. She was my first love, I don't know where it all went wrong. I thought she'd be as happy as I was about your birth as I was but you've lived the outcome of that. Don't get me wrong I love my wife but I love your mother for giving me a son, Zeek said getting emotional.

The two embraced before Zeek got up to go sit in the car. Malcolm decided to talk to his mom for a while before leaving to go home. **Hi mom, I wish we could have met on good terms. I wish you could've seen me get married and to meet your grandbabies. Best of all I wish you were there to see me graduate from the academy to become the officer I am today. I spend everyday with Serenity because she looks just like you and she's the closest I'll get to knowing you. Grandma and Grandpa are taking care of her but Jamal is doing a good job at being a dad since he was released. I Love You.**

Before Malcolm could stand to leave he heard footsteps behind him and the voice of Serenity shouting; Mally you're here to see mommy too. Turning around he saw Jamal with his hands in his pockets. Yeah munchkin I came to see mommy and I'm going to check on your auntie. Is auntie ok do I need to come see Marquis, Serenity asked with concern?

No you don't need to come play with Marquis right now sis. Your auntie is going to have a baby girl in a few months. That's why I have to see if I need to take her to the doctor early. Then Malcolm walked up to Jamal and shook his hand and got into the car with Zeek to head home.

During the short time that they were in the cemetery Jamal and Serenity sat quietly. Then she noticed her dad was crying all she could think to do was wrap her arms around him. Your mom stole my heart with the news of her pregnancy with you. I never got the chance to tell her how I felt about her before she died. So I guess this is the only way I'll get to talk to her until we meet again, Jamal said sadly through tears. Serenity only knew the stories her grandparents told her about her mom.

Most of the stories were of how much she reminded them of her. One day Serenity hopes to sit down with Zeek to find out his opinion of her mother. She couldn't ask her brother because he's never met her during his lifetime. The two children of Melody Stanton have no connection to her other than her parents. Let's hope their bond stays strong and their Love for one another runs deep in their hearts.

Five days later on **Aug 15th** Dametrius and Jazzlene are celebrating their 4th wedding anniversary. Dametrius brought his wife her favorite breakfast from World Tavern. Waking up Jazzlene rubbed her baby bump and smiled thinking of how great life has been with her husband for the last few years. After breakfast the two went to a lamaze class and had lunch in the park. On the way home they stopped by Travion & Harmony's to hang out.

While at their friends home the two asked for advice on parenting. It all seems scary in the beginning but it gets easier once you have a scheduled routine, Trey said honestly. The moment you hold your child and look into their eyes the bond is formed instantly, Harmony said getting emotional. Yeah man when you guys are alone talk to the babies and start building that bond with them. If you do that within the next two months you'll get to feel those kicks, Trey mentioned excitedly. We did take a lamaze class to calm his nerves about it, Jazz mentioned.

That's great guys keep it up you're going to be great parents in January, Harmony said hugging them the best she could. Since she was at the end of her pregnancy about to have her baby boy in a few weeks. If you'd like you guys can come over here to see how we manage a 4 yr old and a newborn next month, Trey told them. We'll definitely stop by for our parenting lessons next month, Dametrius said with a chuckle

10

(Fall)September 2029

Finally we enter the Fall season on **Sept 1st** we'll hang out with Max who's turning 45. After raising three 6 yr olds you'd think this man is worn out. But not this officer, he has enough energy to keep up with all three of them. He always says: You have to stay in shape to do what I do. Seeing how much her husband loves to work out so Cora decided to surprise him by turning their basement into a personal gym. Surprised isn't the word to describe the look on Max's face. It was more like shock mixed with elation when he walked into the basement.

Out of nowhere Max pulled out his phone and called all the guys to come over. I guess our house will now be where all the police department gets fit. Just seeing my husband happy is the best part of the day for me, Cora thought to herself. And it was adorable seeing Alexander lifting weights with his daddy. By the end of the day Alex was telling his sisters that he was super strong and would protect them just like daddy.

The next day our favorite helper Camille turned 11 and thought she was able to tell everyone what to do. But today **Sept 2nd** she just wanted to hang out with her big sister. Since Harmony is due to have her baby boy in 13 days Camille wanted to be a part of the birth. Camille made it clear that she would be staying with her sister until her nephew is born. With that being said Zeek and Kahlani let the two sisters be happily in each other's embrace on the couch.

13 days later on **Sept 15th** it was finally time to meet the newest member of the family. At 8am Travion was in the kitchen with Camille making breakfast for mommy to be. While eating Harmony doubled over as a contraction hit her sitting at the table. Camille and Heaven were both concerned and asked if it was time to have the baby? No, it's not time yet, that was just the first one we have to wait til they come faster, Harmony told the girls.

The next 6 hrs Heaven and Camille watched Harmony

closely like a hawk. Camille even timed the contractions every time her sister doubled over in pain. By 5pm Harmony cried out for Travion as her water broke while making a snack for the girls. There was no time to get to the hospital so Travion called 911 for an ambulance. While on the phone with the dispatcher Camille and Heaven could be heard in the background asking what they could do.

The dispatcher told the girls all the supplies they would need to deliver the baby. When the girls returned with all the supplies Heaven went to her daddy's side. Both were rubbing Harmony's head telling her to breathe and be brave. Camille was the one being brave as she positioned herself to catch the baby. When the dispatcher told Harmony to push Camille looked down and realized she didn't have any gloves so she ran to get two oven mitts.

After 3 pushes the loud shrill of the newborn baby boy as he enters this new world. Welcome the family **Terrance LeRoy Smith** we are glad you're home with us, Harmony said just as the ambulance arrived. Travion had texted Zeek and Malcolm while the dispatcher was coaching Camille through the delivery. As they were loading Harmony and Terrance into the ambulance the family began to arrive. They followed the ambulance to the hospital and Camille had to let everyone know that she delivered the baby.

11

October 2029

After two weeks of Camille bragging about delivering her nephew it's finally quiet around the house. That now brings us to **October 3rd, a sad** day for Zeek and Harmony. Sitting side by side on the couch Zeek held his new grandson and vented to his eldest daughter. "Your mother would've been 45 today" he said, shedding tears. I wish I could have met her daddy, Harmony replied, getting emotional as well. If only she could have gotten to meet her grandbabies or Harrison.

Yeah that would've been great baby girl but you remind me so much of her. You know your mom was in school to be a teacher when I met her so you being a teacher made her dream come to life. Wow I never knew that about my mom, that makes me feel so much closer to her. Yeah I remember holding you just like this when I picked you up off the porch where she left you. It was the proudest moment for me as a man and father.

I've sat and held each of my children just like this in a nursery and formed a bond with each of you guys. Just like I told Malcolm I'll tell you, I do love my wife but I also love your mother for giving me "You". I do wish your mothers would have formed this same bond with you guys. But I don't want you to hate your mother for the choices your grandfather forced her to make. That was new to Harmony because again she never knew anything about her mother.

But 14 days later the family got together on **Oct 17th** to visit baby Terrance. They also wanted to hang out with 4 yr old Heaven as she held her little brother or her little butterball as she likes to call him. The whole day Heaven played the role of mommy to her brother in front of everyone. You can easily tell that little girl loves that baby more than her own toys. She wants to help change him, give him a bath and feed him.

Once all this love has been spread throughout this month the only way to close it out is with some more. Lastly on **Oct 25th** Regina turns 43 and is proud of it. Lincoln and Rashad wanted her to feel like a Queen the whole day. After breakfast it was off to work where Regina found a box of her favorite chocolates and a card in her homeroom. The card came from Lincoln who wrote

Mommy

You're the best mommy for me and all the kids at school say they want a mommy like mine. You taught me how to write so I could be the smartest student in kindergarten. Daddy said you are the prettiest lady in the world and I agree. Love you mommy

Lincoln

By lunchtime Rashad came by to have some time with his wife before returning to his shift. The two sat in the courtyard to split a tray from World Tavern. All of the students stopped by to say "Happy Birthday" which made her smile. The two agreed to have the chocolates at home after dinner. When she went back into the building Regina put the chocolates in the fridge of the staff room. In her haste Regina forgot to put a note on it so Kahlani put one on it for her.

At the end of the day after grabbing the chocolates out of the lounge Regina stopped to talk to Cora and Kahlani in the parking lot. I Love you guys, you are the best friends a girl could ever ask for, Regina stated getting emotional. You even introduced me to a great man that I couldn't find on my own. Let me stop you right there sis, Kahlani led us to two great men that take good care of us, Cora replied. Now head on home to see what else your husband has in store for you, Kahlani answered with a sly smile. After hugging her friends Regina made her way to her car and headed in the direction of her home.

When she arrived home both Lincoln and Rashad were standing at the front door. As she got out of the car she could see the candles lit in the house. By the time Regina got up the stairs Lincoln was jumping up and down with excitement to see her. Mommy did you like my card. I had aunt Cora put it in your classroom for me. I loved it handsome and it made mommy happy all day, Regina replied. Once in the house Lincoln asked if his mom would tuck him into bed.

While tucking Lincoln into bed Regina asked why he wasn't eating dinner with them. Lincoln replied: daddy already fed me and gave me a bath, we were just waiting for you to get home. Okay baby rest well and sweet dreams, Regina spoke as she gave her son a kiss on the forehead. After changing her clothes Regina made her way back downstairs to find Rashad standing in the kitchen with two plates of food. Surprised, she asked: who cooked all of this? With a chuckle Rashad replied: Chef Jean walked me through it over a Zoom call.

Wow I hope he teaches you and Max some other recipes to eat around here. Yeah baby he said we could call him anytime for help, so stop talking and try the food for me please, Rashad asked. Without another word Regina picked up a fork full of the fried rice and a piece of the smothered chicken. Impressed by the taste Regina leaned over to give Rashad a kiss before diving back into her plate.

After dinner Rashad brought over a slice of Strawberry

cheesecake for his wife and one for himself. She looked a little put off by the fact that he sat two plates on the table. Rashad looked at her with a smirk saying: I know better than to eat off your plate so I got my own plate. Ok she answered with a chuckle as she placed a fork full into her mouth.

In an instant "Mmm" was all Regina could say about the taste of the cheesecake. Did Chef Jean teach you to make this as well? Yes he did baby and I'm guessing by your reaction it was good, Rashad replied. Good it was delicious hubby I hereby request that you make this again, Regina stated stuffing her face.

After the two finished their candlelight dinner and dessert Rashad told Regina to get ready for bed while he cleaned up. Regina did as she was told and found a bubble bath awaiting her upstairs. After soaking for a while Regina felt the fingers of her husband pushing the hair from her face as he put it in a ponytail for her. With her eyes closed Regina thought: this man is so good to me I have to do something nice for him next month.

12

November 2029

We've come to the end of the Fall season and it will tug at your heartstrings. Harmony looked at the calendar noticing that it was **Nov 5th** the day her favorite author **K.Moore** turns 47. Harmony found out that K.Moore was having a book reading of her next novel at the library. It was a must that she meet her favorite author in person. Before leaving work she called Trey asking him to pick up the kids so she could go to the book reading.

Just as she arrived at the library Harmony noticed that her family was there as well. It made her happy to see her husband and kids were there to support her tonight. During the book reading Harmony took notes as people asked questions. At the end Harmony and her family went up to get autographs and photos with K.Moore.

When they arrived home Harmony told Travion this was one

of the things she could check off her bucket list. She kissed both of her children before putting them to bed. Then she went to the master bedroom where she laid next to her husband in a warm embrace. Travion watched his wife sleep with a smile on her face and all he could think was: it feels good just to see her happy.

Four days later on **Nov 9th** Crystal Jameson would be 44 on this day. This was a really bittersweet day for Christian as a man. To know his mother died while bringing him into the world makes him sad. Even though he grew up with Kahlani as the mother figure in his life he still loves his biological mother in his heart. It would have been great to see his mom on his wedding day even at his graduations.

Sitting in his apartment with his new wife Christian was in deep thought of the woman he never met. Sitting out in the living room Christian began to pray and talk to Crystal.

Dear Heavenly father

Thank you for giving me this great family that's kept me safe all these years. Thank you for the beauty that just married me 4 months ago. I pray that someday you'll bless us with a family of our own. Mom I don't know why you didn't want me when I was conceived. Just know that as your son I still love you in my heart. You'd love Ma. She took great care of me and my older siblings. I hope when we meet in the resurrection that you will welcome me with open arms. In Jesus name

Amen

Seeing her husband in turmoil Desiree placed her arms around his shoulders. She whispered in his ear: I know today is hard for you. I'm here if you wanna talk about it. Just hearing his wife say those words made him feel a lot better.

After this touching moment three days later on **Nov 12th** Rashad turns 45. Before heading to the station Rashad received breakfast from his wife and son. And he found a note on his dashboard from his wife:

Hey birthday boy

I'll be having a treat delivered to the station for you around lunchtime. Don't worry I don't mind if you share with the boys. I also have a surprise for you when you get home tonight. Have a good day and please be safe.

Wifey

Rashad couldn't wait until his lunch break on that day and all the guys wondered what had him so excited. Once 11:30 arrived a delivery from World Tavern arrived at the door for him. Rashad knew his wife placed this order because it was filled with all his favorite foods. When Zeek and Max noticed the food in the lobby they went to grab a plate for themselves. Next Malcolm walked in and said: Hey uncle Max, uncle Shad, hey pop what's going on in here.

Your aunt Regina bought lunch for the whole station today,

Max replied. So Malcolm grabbed a plate for himself and socialized with his co-workers until it was time for his shift to start. Once lunch was over Rashad knew Regina was in class so he sent her a text.

Hey baby

Thank you for lunch today. All the staff enjoyed it as much as I did. I can't wait to see you tonight . Have a good day and I Love You

Shad

While on patrol Rashad received a text from his wife replying to his text from earlier.

Hey hubby

Sorry I didn't get back to you earlier but you're most welcome. You can tell the rest of the team I said You're Welcome. I can't wait to see you tonight handsome. Have a safe shift and I'll see you later

Gina

By 7pm Rashad finally made it home to his family where Lincoln was washing his plate after eating. On his way to his room Lincoln stopped to tell Rashad that he helped mommy make dinner for that night. Then there was Regina standing by the table with his plate of dinner in hand. After placing the food down on the table she motioned for Rashad to have a seat which he complied. There's no need to say anymore we all know how the rest of this night went.

Two weeks later we come to everyone's favorite time of shenanigans with Janette. Everyone gathered at Zeek and Kahlani's as they do every year. This **Nov 25th** was no different with Janette and her antics. Upon entering the house Janette started telling the story of how the cashier at the grocery store tried to overcharge her for a Honey Baked Ham a week ago. What did you do Ma, Zeek asked with a heavy sigh? Son, chill out I just asked for the manager who told me I was being overcharged and helped me with my purchase.

So you didn't act a fool in that store in front of Pop, Kahlani asked with a raised brow. Well just let me explain daughter that my actions were very necessary. That girl told me that my husband would be happier with her than with me, so I turned the other cheek. But when she threw a roll of pennies and the other ham I didn't buy at the back of my head. I yoked her up in front of the manager and dragged her outside for that much needed beating which she received from me.

There wasn't a dry eye in that house for the rest of the night thanks to Janette. Ma just putting up with you makes me want you and Pop to go have a session with Dr. Matthews, Zeek stated. We'll all go with you for a group session if you'd like, Kahlani agreed with Zeek.

Message from the Author

Thank you guys for following this saga of my characters Leaving their trauma behind. As we just concluded a fun year with the cast we'll be moving on in another direction to overcome trauma. I'm sure you're all aware that addiction can have a very powerful hold on everyone. In this series some are addicted to Love and Janette is addicted to being a hilarious Karen in public. So in the next book all of our couples will be having couples counseling for a year.

Maybe Janette will get better with her Karen activities but we'll have to wait and see. We will also be welcoming 3 new babies courtesy of Kapri and Jazzlene as well. So prepare yourself for therapy and healing in **Marriage Anonymous.**

Contact Me

Email: relatablefictionwriting@gmail.com

Facebook:nakeialdavis-moore

Instagram: soultavern_owner2020

Tik Tok: Leavingtrauma4

www.ingramcontent.com/pod-product-compliance
Lightning Source LLC
LaVergne TN
LVHW012036060526
838201LV00061B/4637